CW00434919

DREAMS OF LIFE

poetry pt today

DREAMS OF LIFE

Edited by Rebecca Mee

First published in Great Britain in 1999 by Poetry
Today, an imprint of
Penhaligon Page Ltd, Remus House, Coltsfoot Drive,
Woodston, Peterborough. PE2 9JX

© Copyright Contributors 1999

All rights reserved. No part of this publication may be
reproduced, stored in a retrieval system, or transmitted
in any form or by any means, without prior permission
from the author(s).

A Catalogue record for this book is available from the
British Library

ISBN 1 862 26598 4

Typesetting and layout, Penhaligon Page Ltd, England.
Printed and bound by Forward Press Ltd, England

Foreword

Dreams Of Life is a compilation of poetry, featuring some of our finest poets. This book gives an insight into the essence of modern living and deals with the reality of life today. We think we have created an anthology with a universal appeal.

There are many technical aspects to the writing of poetry and *Dreams Of Life* contains free verse and examples of more structured work from a wealth of talented poets.

Poetry is a coat of many colours. Today's poets write in a limitless array of styles: traditional rhyming poetry is as alive and kicking today as modern free verse. Language ranges from easily accessible to intricate and elusive.

Poems have a lot to offer in our fast-paced 'instant' world. Reading poems gives us an opportunity to sit back and explore ourselves and the world around us.

Contents

December Spring

In a Winter bleak and dreary,
When spirits were quite low;
Came a sudden change quite cheery -
Sunshine instead of snow.

Five days of heavenly sunshine,
Unseasonably warm;
Blue skies, light breeze and air like wine,
So nice after the storm.

There also came upon the scene,
A lady to inspire
The likes of me, who could have been,
Stuck firmly in the mire.

The mire of boredom with my lot
And loneliness as well.
But then the scene changed like a shot -
The lady cast her spell.

Her bubbling personality,
Quick wit and humour too,
Surmounted our banality -
Inspiring us anew.

So active and energetic,
An outdoor type for sure;
Most certainly sympathetic,
Her qualities endure.

Her irrepressible laughter
Spreads happiness around:
So much that forever after -
Fond memories abound.

My now quite steadfast devotion,
To her is plain to see.
And barely hidden emotion
Means that she's loved by me.

A O Jones

England In Spires

At dusk I stroll a quiet Cotswold lane until at houses' end,
Beside a meadow fence I pause, before a gentle scene
That beckons like a friend.

Close by, dark brindled ponies graze.
Beyond, cloud fleeced sheep stand listening
To nature's evensong.
Farther still, at meadow's end above the towering trees
A shining steeple rises tall,
Dressed in golden rays, against the darkening sky.

I linger dreaming of bells and chimes,
Of white-robed angelic choirs,
Their lips moon-shaped and uplifted radiant eyes.
Majestic organ forests and thundering hymnal winds.

'Tween oaken pews, on rainbow cushions bright
Embroidered with cross and dove and crown,
Silent figures kneel to pray
Palms pressed, fingers stretched, arms raised -
Hand spires - vectors pointing Home.

Oh England, your landscape crests in flèches,
Where weary, winged travelers light,
Where Holy Spirit hovers heeding songs and tears below,
Where proud knees bend and burdened souls find rest.
A stalwart spire our tripping thoughts and hurried lives arrests.

Steeple masts, above the storm-tossed waves, above the currents that
betide us -
Stone sentinals tall, immutable, ancient guardians keeping watch,
Body forth God's presence eternal through war and unbelief.

Above farm, tree and roof,
Silhouette against the gathering dark,
A slender spire joins earth and sky,
And through the cross below
Unites our lives with Him.
These arrows to the promised Place direct our eyes above,
And through His Spirit we're filled with perfect Love.

In that day when spires no longer we see,
With new eyes beholding Him we'll be in ecstasy.
For now, this Highest One our mast, stronghold, resting place,
Not spire reflecting sunlit mirror,
But brightest most glorious star in darkest day.
For endless ages Christ, our Light, our Life, our Way.

Nina Helene

Second Chance

It's thirty years since last we met, almost to the day,
Not since my wife, her sister, passed away,
I can't believe my eyes, nor credit what I see,
There stands the dream I loved and lost, the very epitome.

Her lovely smile, her tone of voice, her laughter, her tears,
So reminiscent of the sounds I knew, music to my ears,
The way she walks, the way she talks, I've seen and heard before,
Her manner, her demeanour, there's more, and more, and more.

A light that dimmed, extinguished, so many years ago,
Suddenly, inexplicably, again began to glow,
I've re-discovered what was lost, I've walked down memory lane,
And found that what I loved back then, is there to love again.

Don't know her all that well, I've been away so many years,
What she likes, how she's lived, her hopes, her dreams, her fears,
I don't suppose she looks on me, as other than a brother,
Her one true love has passed away, could she love another?

They'd lived and loved together, built a nest for two,
Would it be unfaithful, to care for someone new?
She'd done her very best for him, solicitously giving,
Remember him, then given time, remember life's for living.

Am I wishful thinking, of how life used to be?
And I just an ageing fool, sees what he wants to see?
I know my life will never, ever, be the same again,
The joy, the bliss, euphoria, it's driving me insane.

Until that fateful day we met, I'd settled for my lot,
How could I know that fickle fate, would fire a parting shot,
Many things in this old life, are not as they may seem,
Hope springs eternal, for I have found my dream.

Jim Storr

Love Is A Gift From God

Love is when Christmas Church bells ring,
Love is when our hearts do sing.

Love is remembering a shining star,
Love is remembering wise men from afar,
Love is remembering them guided by its light.
Love is remembering baby Jesus that night.

Love is remembering where baby Jesus lay,
Love is remembering he was in a manger, laid on hay.
Love is remembering Jesus was the Christ child,
Love is remembering *why* the wise men smiled.

Love is why Christmas Church bells now ring,
Love is why our hearts should always sing.

Sheryl Williamson

Love Is . . .

Love is . . .
A baby's first smile to proud mum and dad
A new born calf to a farmer so glad
A bride and groom on their happiest day
A guide dog leading the blind on their way
A mother hugging her child with care
A promise to say you will always be there
A hand to hold when you're so alone
Even a tender word over the phone
It's hearing your child say 'Mum I love you'
It's a kiss in return for the nice things you do
It's caring for someone too old to bend
It's when your daughter says 'Mum, you're my friend'
Love is when your grandchild is on his way
When he's placed in your arms, the very first day
Love is not seen but you know it's there
The security, need and wanting to care
Love is for all to have and it's free
Love is out there, for you and for me!

C Freeman

It's You

It's you who breathed life into my lifeless life,
You who gave thoughts
For my thoughtless mind,
And you brought joy into my empty eyes.

You gave me love for my loveless heart,
Strength for my arms,
Make my stomach taut,
Now I must thank you,
And just want to say,
'Come live inside me,
And guide me today.'

D Sawyer

Reflection

As I reflect on my past years
I look to the future with hope
A new chapter in my life is starting
I used to look at my reflection and think of what we had.

I thought we had it all, everything was perfect, we were happy
We had found something special that only others
Dreamt about.
I gave you my all, for what?
You turned against me, threw it all in my face . . . your lies
Your guilt, your deceit . . . your definition of love.
Nothing was ever good enough, you always wanted more
Too afraid to lose me, always thinking you were missing out
I was always thinking I was losing . . . someone special to me.
No one was allowed to see me, I was yours
Not to be shared
But I had to share you.

I always put you first and me second . . . so did you
I expressed affection . . . you did not
I offered you warmth . . . you showed me cold
I showed interest in you . . . you did not in me
I treated you with love . . . you took me for granted
I showered you with gifts . . . you didn't bother
I was there for you . . . where were you for me?

I stepped back one day
I realised I was no one to you
Someone to use when it suited you
One rule for you and another for me
I didn't know any different and nor did you
Now I'm free no longer in the dark
I can speak, enjoy life
Be loved for who I am, and liked for my uniqueness
I'm ready to bring love into my life
To be held, cared for, understood and respected
Ready to trust again, no lies, no pain.
I gave my all to someone I didn't know at all

Someone who didn't know what they wanted, never happy with what
they had
To show and feel love through pain is wrong
Tenderness, compassion, intimacy . . . all words with no meaning to
you
You are an unhappy, empty, unfulfilled person
You lack the strength to change
You keep going round in circles.
Make plans, dreams, a reality . . . go for it!
People should be there for each other
Lovers, friends, partners
Look at the person at your side . . . me.

Supporting, loving, sharing good and bad times
Laughing together, not at each other.
We need each other
I want no other
My love for you will last forever.
Let's stay together!

Sonya 'B'

Love Is

Love is the quickening of a heartbeat
When the love of your life you first meet.

Love is the warmth of a new-born child first held
Love is the comfort from a neighbour's child,
Who brings wild flowers freshly picked
Saying 'is your headache better now'
Giving one a loving hug and smile.

Love is all around the world
If only people would feel it's warmth.
Love happens not only when people are happy
But when the unexpected comes into one's day.
Love is the tender touch
From one's spouse, when life has become too much.
Love is in the beauty of the garden
Smelling on a damp summer's night the perfume
Of roses, jasmine and sweet honeysuckle.

Love is the companionable silence between a couple
By the warm fireside on a cold winters night,
When darkness fills the sky and shuts out the light.
Love is the gift from God to everyone on earth
To reach out and say, Love is at the heart of my hearth.

Kathleen Collins

Growing Old

Growing old goes round and round
with *God's* help
we arrive there
and find old *age* is a gem
a gem to be treasured.
Arrival there
is a mighty privilege
Old Age comes
Old Age grows and communicates,
it has the right of way
to places near and far,
as the evening of life comes
heartache and misfortune
may come along the way
sometimes all that is left
is the attachment
to loving and faithful friends
giving great joy in life
freeing old agers
from soul-destroying loneliness.
The old slips away
giving place to the new
most old agers
keep pace with the new
cramping monotony around old age
the dimmed glimpses into twilight
strangle both heart and mind
cripple every effort of will
if old agers allows it.
Thank the *Lord* it doesn't!
So going on to struggle happily and peacefully.
Keeping old age dignified
and lucrative.

K Kent

Vacant Chairs

As I look across our tiny room
I see your empty chair,
and as I sit and stare at it,
I imagine you're still there,
as I watch the firelight
and the flames that gently sway
I sit and think of how things were
and I dream of yesterday . . .

We had a life that was happy
and we lived from day to day,
although we had our ups and downs
our problems didn't stay,
then I remember a particular time
one sunny day in May,
when we were walking hand in hand
that God took you away.

As I wake up from my dream
I feel the tears upon my cheek,
I know my time is nearly up
and my maker I will meet,
then I shuffle across the room
to sit upon your chair
I feel your arms around me
and I know that you are there . . .

Now I'm, walking in God's beautiful garden
with the one that I still love,
I see a ray of heavenly light
that shines from up above,
so when you think about time
please don't shed those tears,
for I am where I want to be even though there's vacant chairs.

Kathleen Tutty

Miaow!

When someone said: 'You're getting old'
I wondered what they meant.
    My stride may not be quite so brisk,
    My sight not so acute;
But my stamina puts her to shame -
I still stand tall, while she is bent.

I am no clinging vine - not I!
While she seeks vainly for a man
I let them come to me.
And when I need a helping hand
A friend will always see:
    And if I should appear a little bit unsteady,
    A door is always opened, a strong arm always ready.
The years roll by, the bones may ache,
But mind and spirit still are strong.

Younger by a dozen years,
But settled in her ways,
She may not have the tranquil heart
To keep her hopeful all her days.
To be a pessimist is sad,
Mean spirit even worse;
But still I do not wish her ill,
I hope she will not feel the chill
Of unkind words if someone says:
    'You're getting old.'

E D Sulston

An Old Stager

I'm now in the twilight of my life
A Sexagenarian of sixty-three,
It's proving to be a terrific time
As now I can plan for just me!

When I was a child I was always told what to do
Next I was a very inhibited Teenager.
But now that I've become a Senior Citizen
At last I'm a bit of a Rager!

For the first time in my life
I can tell folk 'Take a hike'
I don't suffer fools gladly
And I can do as I like.

You're just as old as you feel
This adage suits me
I take full advantage of everything
And I now have lots of freedom, you see.

I took Early Retirement
Over six years ago.
Then I wrote down all the things
That I'd always wanted to know.

A Correspondence Course
In Poetry Writing came first
As for creating verses
I always had a thirst.

Then I bought a banjo
As I always fancied this instrument,
With a new case to carry it in
Off to Lessons I went.

I joined a Health Club
And went often to the Gym,
A friend took me to the local Baths
Where she taught me to swim.

At fifty-five I had learned to drive
I passed my Driving Test at the second Go
This has been the greatest benefit to me
And give the freedom I never used to know.

Three years ago I took up Line Dancing
And although I may be getting old
I already have my Bronze and Silver medals
And at the end of September I'm going to 'Go for Gold!'

So I consider that in my Retirement
I am having such a lot of fun,
That I can really really recommend 'growing old'
These are only some of the exciting things I have done.

Mary Anne Scott

A Stately Affair

You're as old as you feel
You are never old if you believe
Your goal is to keep ageing need
At bay and what a relief!

One gets forgetful
If you are forced to rush
Around to get to your Fellowship Club
Brush away the quarry be there on time

Be ready to answer the postman's knock
Enjoy your letters to the full
Don't forget to wear your favourite frock
Just be bright, don't feel dull

Gather your wits about you
Tender your heart strings
Do have a good time let your manfriend constantly ring
Bring that stately affair into the light

How brave and courageous not to let yourself grow old
Bring joy into your friend's heart
Be bold and let sunshine right from the start
Shine brightly and step nimbly caring not for ageing fright

Alma Montgomery Frank

Growing Old

Old age just creeps up on you.
It takes you unawares.
One minute you're a busy bee,
The next you're creaking at the knee.
One day you're running for the 'bus,
The next it's 'Let it go. Why fuss.'
They say old age brings wisdom.
I'm sure they're right, and yet,
So many things I used to know
I find I now forget.
Friends start to look much older.
Some even fade away.
But some are still deep down the same
And we can laugh our cares away, just as we always did.
Shopping till you drop takes on a whole new meaning.
I find I sometimes have to pause
To find a seat when out of doors.
But if you can keep the aches away
Old age can be quite fun,
A chance to do the things you want
And go at just the pace that's right
From early dawn till late at night.
Independence is a must if you can manage it.
With friends to share a meal, a chat . . .
A chance to listen and be heard,
Whatever happening has occurred.
It has to come to all of us, this stage
We call 'old age',
But I'm not ready for it yet.
I'll wait a while until I get
Much older. *Much* older!

P M Jay

17

Old

Life at times is wearisome when you're growing old
Although I suppose you can get away
with being cheeky, rude or bold.
No one really thinks that you are sensible anymore,
and at times I'm sure they think you are just a great big bore.

The print in all the papers has reduced in size you know,
why can't they print it larger, like they used to years ago.
And why can't TV pictures be as clear as when first came out.
As they have a captive audience there's no need to worry about -
Giving us clear pictures, I suppose now anything will do,
And why do eye hole needles have to be so small now too.

I really cannot understand why all these things have changed.
Is it economics, or just I'm going strange?
Maybe it is what is known as second childhood once again,
Like the thrill and excitement from toys, puzzles and steam trains.
Do I have to be so treated, like a baby that's spoonfed,
Washed and dressed by someone - when I feel inside my head -
I can do things for myself, like wash my face and comb my hair,
Dress myself and put my shoes on - *once I get out of my chair!!!*

E M Budge

Memories

Seventy years ago, my dearest,
I was young and gay.
Joyful I played, my laugh the clearest
All the live long day.
Morn brought delight, no trace of sadness,
Life seemed one endless spring.
Light as a bird, in youthful gladness
I used to dance and sing -
I, who am old and grey.

Seventy years to come, my dearest,
You will be old and grey.
Death will have seized your loved and nearest,
Age tramps a lonely way.
What will you do when old, my fairest?
Live in the past once more?
See then of memories the rarest
You have a golden store -
You who are young and gay.

M W Lee

Seventy-One

My sight is blurred, hearing too,
I've fitted the glasses, it helps a lot,
the hearing aid made the world a place
of cacophony and loud noise,
they say you can switch it off
if you can find the switch!
Tales of age make them turn away,
if you walk your joints ache, creak,
to button clothes when fingers fumble.
Then a smile, a helping hand, a voice
that you can hear, as he
knows the need to shout,
so your past and future is discussed
and laughed about.
This makes a day bearable once more.

Tom Hern

The Ageing Process

Things that once would never have fazed me,
Now seem to give me so much stress,
Is this all perfectly normal?
Is it part of the ageing process?
Days have now become so tiring, but
I'm not really dozing in front of the TV,
Like my mother, years ago, used to say,
I'm merely resting my eyes, you see.

How I love a shopping spree,
I prefer to shop on my own,
But recently that's not been the case,
Now I rarely go alone,
I can't read the print on packages etc,
So without my glasses or a friend along,
I seem to misinterpret the instructions,
Or choose the sizes all wrong.

I even wear glasses when cooking now,
If not I use the wrong regulo number,
Then burnt offerings appear on the menu,
Whilst I chalk up yet another blunder,
I can't actually see much without them,
So I wear my glasses most of the time,
Is the print really getting smaller,
Or is it just another ageing sign?

Creaking knees whenever I bend,
Aching joints by the close of day,
Varicose veins from standing too long,
As you can see I'm well on my way
To getting my pension and bus pass,
I'm just waiting for these concessions to start,
But it wouldn't seem quite so bad,
If I didn't feel so young at heart.

Anne Williams

Growing Old

This is a terrible concept
Bestowed on us by those who are young.
And the age we enter our dotage
Becomes earlier as life moves along
You never admitted to old age
Whilst you still had a job
But now, once you've reached forty
You're suspect and put on the back hob.
But who do the young feel they can turn to
When they are really in need?
Looking for words of wisdom
Their dented ego to feed.
Old age is still for living,
There's special tasks still for you.
The purpose you were born to fulfil
Doesn't end until you are through.
Old age is only a trick of the mind
'With my legs . . . what *can* I do?'
You lived and thrived before you could stand
So what's so different now?
We each one were born with the spirit of life
Urging us forward each day
Making us fearless - eager - alive.
So don't you ever say
'Sorry my dear - can't do that now -
I'm growing old you see.'
Turn - 72 - into - 27 - stay young at heart like me.

Irene Spencer

Alone Again

A slap a sudden wail, another cry in the dark
Warmth smooth nuzzled goodness first taste of bliss,
A solitary journey, aching pushing strive to embark.
Sudden light, laughter, joy in a mother's loving kiss.

Walking through the forbidding gates of life
Fear of the unknown, buildings, shouting children, stern unbending
             teachers.
Maybe academic success or years of misery and strife.
Exams, lectures the ups and downs that govern one's future.

Puberty, much unsure fumbling, nights of unrequited passion.
Those probing lessons untaught, yet eagerly learnt by all
Experiments with drugs and sex, pushed by trendy fashions.
Doubts, questions, some unanswered as we stumble gamely after
             nature's call.

Overtaken by years of hurt and soul destroying, mindless toil.
Our partners and friends lost memories in battered photo albums.
What pulled, nay dragged one towards that ultimate, inevitable goal
Our fate already sealed, water, earth, air ourselves become as one.

T Bates

Us

Of dreams we see but cannot tell
Of quiet times we both know well
Where memories and feelings are truly stored
Bridges built o'er gaps and river's ford
I come to you

A silent whisper deep in my ear
Brings a peace to me that allays all fear
Of days to be their ends I don't see
There you are hidden so deep in me
My love to be

You hold me untiring in your arms
I am accepted in your upturned palms
With rainbow feelings caught in morning dew
Those three words of silence I share with you
Be with me now

There are many dreams that may come true
Then those loving thoughts of me and you
Only time to come will see the end
Of those wishes and dreams I know not when
I belong to you

Is there a time just for me and you
Will there be something for our love so true
Have we always to stay here deep inside
To love in our souls wherein we hide
My time for you

I feel flower soft whispers on my skin
Your strength a crystal tower has been
I have precious things of yours I hold
Your words and feelings won't grow old
In my soul you be

Your rainbows end with it's golden trove
Arcs over joining our minds with love to grow
We on did go soul within soul for us to know
Our separate ways and paths are joined just so
Our love we know

Your love must leave lots of room for others
That the feelings we have must never smother
The space that only needs you to fill
This sun moves aside but loves you still
A space for me

We are both asked of us here inside
To let go but the tears they cannot hide
That in the end not as friends we know
I will in love never be able to let you go
I love you so

Yenti

Love Is A Feeling

Love is a feeling, that is hard to explain
Like the hot summer sun or the cold winter rain
It can make you so happy, it can make you so sad
But most of us think it's the best feeling we've had

A day seems so endless when you are apart
This thing called love, pulls the strings to your heart
To lay in their arms or the lingering kiss
Such strong emotions, you can't bear to miss

The sound of their voice, makes you weak at the knees
Butterflies in your stomach, just seeming to tease
You can't sleep at night, you toss and you turn
For their warm embrace, your body does yearn

You're unable to think or concentrate on your work
The loneliness of love, it really can hurt
Love is contagious, it can make you feel ill
But there's no simple cure like taking a pill

Back together again, let the passion begin
Their soft gentle caress, lights the fire within
Such happiness is found, your heart starts to sing
What a wonderful feeling, true love can bring

Linda Brown

Autumn

Streets hushed, faintly misty
Kids' voices far away
Wet fallen leaves on gardens, railings
A darkening in the air
A sense of quiet, of being over.

Autumn brings thoughts of ageing
Youth's spring long gone, and the grown-up summer years
The past now more important than the future
And recollected endlessly
(Through alienation from the modern world
Phones that talk back, cellophane on everything, and
'sorry, we've had problems with our computer')
There's only memory - through many autumns -
Even the bad bits seeming better
The unfolding pageant of one unimportant life
The strange beauty of its odd turns and flourishes
And brooding on what might have been instead.

Your life. Just the once. Never again.
Autumn promises the year will end
Yet be renewed
But you won't.

M G Sherlock

Mementoes Of Life

Old age is a fading reflection of one's former self
All one has to show for life are mementoes on one's shelf
Minute by minute, life surely ebbs away
How long anyone has, who can truly say?

We are passengers in time, travelling here and there
The beginning does so excite, the end does so scare.
We try our utmost to achieve what we can in between
Our mementoes remind us what we have done and been.

Youth and middle age, neither of which for long lingers
Like water, each trickles so quickly between our fingers
The opposite ends of life's spectrum are old age and our prime
If life is a ladder, then mememtoes are the steps we climb.

Asif Ali

Reluctant Surrender

I am at war!
A losing, hopeless war!
No blood is spilled, no one is killed
Though strong and cruel is the foe.
It can't be heard, it can't be seen
But lurks there behind the scene.
A potent army in silent lines
Marches each day; it burrows trenches
On soft, defenceless prey.
It settles
Invading, deranging, decaying,
Wilting, tainting and fading
Colours, beauty, spirit and love.
Nowhere to run, no place to hide,
No saints to hear your prayers.
Superfluous and futile
Is the chemical weapon's pile.
Yet I fight!
I fight hard and more
Alas, it is in sight,
It's at my door, I must surrender.
You win Old Age
Here I am;
Please be gentle, please be tender.

Carolina Rosati-Jones

Growing Old Gracefully

When young you assert you have no wish to grow old,
For you say that's when you'll be left out in the cold.
Not if you always keep a sunny face,
And practise those little things which lead to grace.

It is said that growing old can be a bind,
And that's when the bones begin to grind.
But though many shackles come to dismay you,
Go blithely along and meet each day anew.

Not too blithely of course, you have an example to set,
Try to be happy - so that the young ones don't fret.
Do any chosen work quietly and you will find,
It leads to that cherished peace of mind.

You may not be showered with glory,
But you will always have your own simple story.
To comfort you when things are dulled by pain,
And you may think how nice it would be to be young once again.

Betty Green

Closing Chapters

I am wondering
at the Concorde speed,
the devil-may-care,
reckless race
of Time.
I am wondering
how long I may just
sit by, ruminating
on the pulsating passage
of months
that pitilessly
pass me by,
minute hands beating
on drums within my skull,
and long curtains closing
on mute twilights.
I am wondering
why that which is left
in life
seems to be at the
pawnbrokers
and it is my show place
where I peer
cataract-eyed,
fanatically
through thicknesses of glass
at borrowed,
infinitely precious opportunity
and I cannot help wondering,
hustled in dismay,
hurtling dazedly through
days like ashes
how I could have
once, maybe yesterday,
wanted desperately
to die.

Ruth Daviat

Pension Scheme

You pay into a pension scheme
To benefit when you retire.
Your aim within your daily work
Is in position to get much higher.
You strive to buy a property
And pay large mortgage sums.
You have a wife and family
And accept all that comes.
You lose your job at sixty
So benefits you have to claim.
To forfeit your home a pity
But you try to remain sane.
You find rented accommodation
Thanking God you're still alive,
And struggle on with trepidation
Hoping you'll reach sixty-five.
At last the year is upon you
So now to live with ease,
But benefits you no longer get
And to exist is quite a squeeze.
You paid into a pension scheme
To benefit when you retire,
But alas it was a dream
It's all paid back to those that hire.

D Thomas

Growing Old

Growing old? I do not like it,
Perhaps maturing, yes, I think
That is better, like good wine
Not mature? Not fit to drink,

Have a hobby, you're not useless
Knit or paint, do exercise
Help at Christmas in the kitchen
What about home-made mince pies?

Do not tell your grown up offsprings
What to do, you can advise
If they ask you, but be tactful
Then maybe they will think you're wise

And turn to you when they're in trouble
If they don't, you mustn't be
Hurt, you always must be patient
Then they'll come, just wait and see,
Mature in wisdom then you'll be
A friend to all your family.

Valerie Peers

My Only Love

You are my jewel,
In this landscape of beauty.
Which is ever lost in time,
Hauntingly beautiful and unspoilt.
You are my only love.
With the touch of tears,
I could sail to the sun.
The voyage back, to eternity,
I would surely want to run.
As you are my only love,
The rhythm of my life.

E Perrin

Seeking Life

For many years she walked the path of darkness
Seeking life, its very source to find.
She wished for love and to her it was granted,
Stranglehold about her it entwined.

An albatross about her neck was hanging
Heavy as lead; she wished that she was dead.
Like Midas she did seek the source of Pactolus,
There, these words to light her soul were fed.

That he who loves and seeketh not receiveth,
Give and life will be your gift, so chaste.
As jewels in the summer's early morning
Gleamed these words of wisdom in sun's rays.

'Give, and it will be given to you - ' Luke 6:38

Pauline Dodworth

Still My Girl

Daughter mine, where did you go?
Surely not so far away.
You are not the girl I used to know,
I knew you could not stay.
It makes me feel so very old,
To see you fully grown.
When I gave you life, I was not told,
You would only be on loan.
Sometimes I see, with a glimmer of hope,
The child within you still,
When you get upset, and have a mope,
Or when you are feeling ill.
If I dig down really deep,
Or try to get under your skin,
Perhaps catch you when you have a weep,
Yes, underneath you are still my kin.
You may not need me quite as much,
As you did when you were a child,
But I can still give that tender touch,
Which you need when you feel wild.
And your mother needs you more these days,
Than she ever did before.
Whatever may happen, whatever she says,
Now it is my turn, I need you more.

Kim McIntosh

Surroundings

Sky ocean sea blue,
Smoke sewerage weaving its way through,
From pipeless ground it comes
A monster without holding thumbs.

Music blaring enjoyable sounds,
Humans sit suntanning now,
Not to be so whitely dead,
As lifeless souls rising up.

Wind . . . Cool . . . breeze blowing,
Heat off sizzling bodies come,
Earth as well and round our feet.

Water waste, drip away,
I leave this place,
Soon away.

Nothing left,
What was a good place,
Now only in memory time.

Derek Robert Hayes

Fragile Flowers

They are life's fragile flowers,
Who are now in their twilight hours,
Who can't distinguish tomorrow from today,
Yet can remember events like they were yesterday,
There's Elsie who was twenty when the first world war started,
Her fiancé Ted was killed and left her broken-hearted,
Or there's Eric who'd just turn seven,
In the year 1911,
Fred can remember when they shot the Czar,
And even the first motor car,
Now in the autumn of their years,
They await the winter's fears,
While nursey dishes out the 'happy pills',
To keep them cured of all their ills,
The wind blows chill in cold November,
And it's Elsie, Fred and Eric I remember,
Sitting in their bath chairs quite content,
Pondering on their time well spent,
And wondering where the years have went,
Lean on me! Tired old soldier,
Lean upon my youthful shoulder,
There but for God go I,
Passing time until they die
Thinking about when they were still at youth's door,
And when eighty seemed a long time away,
And people were nicer than today,
Perhaps it doesn't matter any more,
These are life's fragile flowers,
With whom we spent many, happy, contented hours.

Alan Pow

Christmas Eve

(For Sally Young)

Sitting at the kitchen table
Larder, cellar out of mind;
Striving, failing to be able
Christmas spirit so to find.

Silent house and log-fire dying
Pours the rain - no star-lit night -
Thoughts of distant kin and trying
Hard to picture their delight.

Suddenly there was a tapping
At the outer darkened door.
With a start I ceased from napping
What, I wondered, was in store?

Season's Spirit quickly entered
Bearing gifts in fine array
Placed upon the table, centred,
To be there on Christmas Day.

Skipped the Spirit down the alley
Fast becoming out of sight,
And with a final Yuletide sally
Disappeared into the night.

As I turned the lights seemed brighter
Was this true or but a fable?
Suddenly my heart was lighter
Stood the Hyacinth on the table.

D P J Smith

Old

As soon as we are born, we are growing old,
Born to die, this I've been told,
It makes you wonder, why we get old,
Made senile, body parts start to wear out,
Being scared, when once so bold,
It's really quite frightening, getting old,
Looking back over the years,
Seeing all the changes about you,
Getting old, does it have any pleasure,
Getting old, it makes you feel blue,
Getting old, I hope so,
Don't you?

Diane Campbell

Age

Age, relativity. Inspiration and creativity.
How much do we inherit?
Upon whose shoulders does the burden sit
For my life? On mine,
Or is it my father's responsibility - actions of his line.
How far back must you go to go forward?
What is the reason for a child who is wayward.

How about suicide? The parents cried.
Do they blame themselves for their child's demise?
Surely, it is not their fault that this world I despise.
They are to be commended for getting me this far.
Pipe into the exhaust of their car.

Yet if as they do, they congratulate me and pride themselves
On their part in my success, must that not mean they share the blame
if I fail?

Iain Henley

41

Being Sensible

It's a fact you don't lessen fun
If your life you sensibly run
No getting into a rut for me
The changes happened naturally
In winter no open coat does flap
In warm clothes I carefully wrap
If it's wet and the wind does blow
I cancel appointments and another time go
Loud and clear I state my grumble
Lately I've noticed how people mumble
I don't waste money or spend it fast
And consider how long my savings will last
I rarely stay out late at night
So in the morning I'm rested and bright
I treat my teeth with extra care
Don't crunch nuts, hard apple or pear
At small print, I no longer peer
When a magnifying glass makes things clear
Yet no one is more surprised than me
Why age should be associated with acting carefully

Joyce Atkinson

Drifting

In a confused forest of images
Her mind wanders,
Having broken loose
From the bonds that attached it to reality.
No longer fretting about past injuries,
She drifts in her vacuum,
Hale, but empty - unburdened at last.

Life had been fraught and disappointing,
So she had escaped into fantasy.
With reality already at arm's length
A fall downstairs in the dark,
A knock on the head, completed the damage.
Now she inhabits a no-man's-land.

Still alive, but no contact can be made
With the woman she once was.
So much has been cut off already,
And she is left with the remnants,
As are we all.

Frail humans have to learn
That here we have no abiding-place,
And that body or mind will break down.
Programmed by her genes to live another decade,
Her mind has not been so strong:
It has already taken leave.
Meanwhile God waits on His threshold
To meet us in our eternal home.

Anne Sanderson

Soliloquy On A Winter's Evening

Things must change; but now I'll rest
Sitting in my chair when I think it's best.
Thinking of today. I'll think of the past,
It was quieter then - today is so fast.
Lottery tickets can now be bought,
Buying such things, one can be caught.
To rely on numbers when you're old,
Is like asking Father Time to withhold
His scythe, so a harvest can be gathered in
And merrymaking made at the local Inn.
Remembering too, that my blood may run
In this battle of life, that cannot be won.
Always I've worked hard to keep my head
When all around me are being bled.
A New Jerusalem was once a choice
Being proclaimed with heart and voice.
Yet dismay fills my heart and home
Dislike too, of that ridiculous *Dome*.

Frank Williams

The Musings Of A Hundred-Year-Old

I'm a hundred-years-old today, my memory is still good,
my brain is A1, my memory is as good as it should,
being still an active fellow, you might like to know,
snow may be on the roof, but there's fire down below,
my birthday cake has twenty-one candles on it - that's nice,
and that's just how many there are on my own slice,
why isn't that nice Dale Winton not married with kids?
and why does 'gay' no longer mean to be happy, as it did,
where are the so called 'erogenous zones'? By me, perhaps?
and why can't I ever find them on any of my maps?
When the Queen Mother is a hundred like me, only a bit shorter,
will she get a birthday letter from her regal daughter?
People ask me if I like sex or violence on TV, or the lack,
in fact I don't, the set-top aerial sticks in my back,
I tried some of that Viagra stuff, as soon as I could,
but sadly, it didn't do my poor arthritis any good,
do you know, I really like Picasso - this is my accolade,
as I have nearly every long playing record he ever made,
my love life really ended when my ardour dropped off,
in my prime about bumping my bits, I couldn't get enough,
if you ever want to know any more about me, I'd rather,
you just might go and start asking my dear old father.

Christopher Higgins

Growing Old

'Yet the inward man is renewed day by day. II Corinthians 4:16b'

Grow old with grace at God's set pace
Then talk each day to Him
For He hath said 'I'll be with you'
E'en as your eyes grow dim.
And if this life gets very hard
God, shall give you more grace,
Family and friends may well forget
You're slowing dawn apace!
You've still got memories to share
Of happy by gone days
Though you're no longer sweet sixteen,
You can your Saviour praise!
And sing those happy songs of yore
Then tell a yarn or two
Which bring a smile, or e'en a tear
But growing old, ain't blue!

Lisa Gore

Growing Old

When people's cars get old, old and worn
    And they begin to toddle.
They go somewhere and trade them in
    And get the latest model

Now I have very often thought
    That when my joints get achy
And when my hair has all turned grey
    And knees are very shaky

And when the onward march of time
    Has left me rather feeble
How nice it would be to find a firm
    That deals in worn-out people

And when my form is bent with age
    And gets to looking shoddy
How nice it would be to turn it in
    And get a brand new body

William Price

Fresh Fields

I've come of age, I'm free at last,
  Thank God I'm free at last;
I've worked, I've waited patiently
  For freedom from the past,
The key of life so rightly earned
  Is now, today, my own:
Tomorrow's door now opens up
  Fresh fields as yet unknown.

The day for which I've often prayed
  Has dawned a subtle glow,
And welcome beams of sunshine's rays
  Now outshine rain or snow;
My world is brighter, lovelier too,
  By far a better place:
I'm free to roam at will as life
  Takes on a diff'rent pace.

No more the race of time and tide
  Of life's created chores,
No more the haste of early start
  To office, bank, or stores:
I'm free at last, I've come of age,
  My freedom's come to stay;
The key's, at last, been handed o'er . . .
  I'm sixty-five today!

Frederick Hays

Lament For Orkney

Gatherings of time-weather stones
A historians delight.
A backdrop of wild, aqua horses
Flowing manes of white.

Look out o'er the Islands
An uncluttered view.
Birds nest in old houses,
Branches are few.

One single set of footprints
Disturb the sand on shore.
Perhaps it'd been a week
Since the shell seeker tread before.

Windows of blood-stained carvings
Line paved streets to invite
Leather envelopes from breast pockets
Of see'ers in awe of the sight.

No rodents competing for the ribbon
The force of the gale is too strong.
Listen to the quiet enchantment
Write words to the rhythmical song.

Karen J Muir

Through The Eyes Of Innocence

A child wanders aimlessly,
Through summer's hazy morn,
Resting in the meadow,
She begins to daydream.

By her side, scattered papers,
Cherished letters from friends,
Words creating vivid pictures,
From far corners of the earth.

With each page I read,
I begin to visualise,
Images all too real,
Through my penpal's eyes.

Over rolling pastures, green and lush,
Chime of cow bells, sounding melodious,
Dulcet tones of goat herders yodelling,
Across low slopes, distantly echoing,
Higher up, as if covered in snows,
Delicate Edelweiss blossoms and grows,
Dotted about are bright-painted chalets,
Window boxes festooned with perfumed flowers.

Oh my friend, I wish you could see,
What this illustration conveys to me.

Snow-capped mountains, towering high,
'Neath a crisp, clear cerulean sky,
Sloping gently to great lake below,
Still and deep with ultramarine glow.
Forests full canopied, tall and serene,
Log cabins scattered throughout the scene,
Many wild animals roaming free,
The bear, the moose and nervous deer.

Oh my friend, I wish you could see,
What this beauty conveys to me.

Torrential rains have quickly passed,
The arid landscape, quenched at last,
Wakened from sleep, plants once dormant,
Painting the dust-bowl with colours vibrant,
Dry, cracked waddies returning to life,
Revitalised from its water-starved strife.

Oh my friend, I wish you could see,
What this transformation conveys to me.

The world is not all adverse,
There are joys to be found,
Through the eyes of innocence,
Wondrous images abound.

Janet Tinkler

Hong Kong

The Towers of Babel climb higher
And higher into the night.
Young lovers and loners haunt the shore
Worshipping the neon shimmers on the river.

Cruisers, ferries and cargo boats pass
Polystyrene flotsam drifts.
While a loud mouthed tourist attention seeks.

Wizened Hakas hunt for aluminium cans.
And DIY fishermen tug at their lines.

Sleepless road drills assault the ear
As the god of Progress
Writhes with Mammon in a sexual union.
Outlying islands are demolished
To feed their offspring:
Concrete and breeze-block.

The need to get there possesses all.
Pushing and shoving.
Barging and rushing.
People-packed masses
Riding on subway trains.

Most are fresh faced office workers
Armed with pagers and mobile phones.
Suddenly one of their number draws
His bleeping weapon to his ear.
Down the mouthpiece he shouts, 'Wah!'
The rest of the mass look down
Jealously pleading at their machines for a call of their own.

Finally they emerge from their subterranean package
To clot streets and shops
With their buying and selling for the world.

Eating out to eat in restaurants.
Where they condemn marine life by pointing.
A panicking turtle surfaces at the top of the tank
For an escape route.
The lobster and the crab
Are bound and gagged.

Air conditioning city heat
To sweat humidity.
Canaries sing and crickets chirp.
Mosquitoes whine with pleasure.

Shrines to gods of the sea.
Shrines to gods of gloried dynasties
Where the old shake sticks in incense clouds
On which a Buddha lotus-floats.
And on either side of the exits and entrances are bells and drums
To sound the alarm.

David A Chamberlain

Leaving Malta, 30th April 1999

Your gently swaying palms waving in the breeze
Your smiling, friendly people always willing to please
Your clear, blue skies and cliffs standing tall
Your sun-kissed shores welcoming all
For the worn out body and weary mind
There's no place like you to relax and unwind
But now it's time for us to part,
Oh Malta, forever will you hold a place in my heart.

Don Wilkinson

Solar Eclipse 1999

To Cornwall we flocked
By car and by train
To view the Eclipse
Which we'll not 'see' again.

We picnicked and partied
As we sat in the park,
Laughing and joking -
And then it grew dark.

People fell silent
At the crescent of light
And effect 'diamond ring',
So awesome the sight.

Nostradamus predicted
The world would now end,
But I am still here,
Writing poems to send.

I'm glad I was there
To join in the fun.
I will always remember
When we lost the sun!

Maria-Christina

City Of Tel Aviv

It's how you remember it that counts
The soft rain is full of evening's warmth
Drifting in from the sea
Caressing the faces
Of promenade walkers.

Coming on.
Strolling, A cool wind cuts
On wide-open backroads of Jaffa.

The days heat, holds only
In the 'Downtown' fabulous circuit
of central Tel Aviv.

Across the Dizengoff
On up Ben Yehudi
Then trotting Allenby
Back down to Dizengoff.

Buying fruit juices by
Colour and fingerpoint,
Drifting through
Open air markets, people babble
And those clutterfull magazine shops.

Finding Banvilles Kepler
In a secondhand store.

In Dizengoff Centre
Dali prints
And girls soldiers sleeping
Breast soft and cheek to cheek,
The confident and the dream-dreamers
Sound in each others arms.

I back-shiver as if God is near.
Makes me reckon this place
Will warm-drift through my space
When most other moorings
Have slipped my memory
Disposable as monkscell mortar.

Patrick Walsh

Broadway

There's a new show in town
That's knockin' them down.
On Broadway.

It's yar to be alive.
And all of that jive.
On Broadway.

Come on along down,
Get hip! Lose that frown.
On Broadway.

Cats move to the sound,
Of the beat on the ground.
On Broadway.

Chicks shimmy and shake,
With the studs on the make.
On Broadway.

See that John in the rain,
Watch him chant for his Jane.
On Broadway.

Stay loose! Lose the blues,
Get a shine on your shoes.
On Broadway.

Dig that crazy old street,
Where the cool people meet.
That's Broadway.

Thomas B Wheatley

Lascaux Caves

This is art at its dawning -
By flick'ring tapers,
In dim and misty ages gone,
In dank recesses of deep caves,
Men drew their world,
And left us richer for their passing.
These were not primitives,
But Men, who knew and loved their land
And lived in tune with it,
Were masters of their universe.
Ours the privilege, ours the gain,
To visit and to share, to glimpse
Those lost ages of our heritage,
And see true beauty.

Roger M Creegan

Travel Log

A world cruise I have to admit is not my scene.
And far distant exotic islands exist only in my daydreams.
I am much impressed with the Yorkshire Dales, and the sleepy
hamlets built of Yorkshire stone.
Also the Lake Districts spectacular scenery always beckons me home.
I can't help but boast of the sandy beaches and sheltered bays of the
West Pembrokeshire coast.
And here on my farm nestled in the hillside I prefer being the most.
I am not very often drawn, or yearn for the big bustling
City of London.
But I feel honoured to be a citizen of the United kingdom.
I remember so well with pleasure my visits to Bonnie Scotland.
Beside the shimmering Lochs and the wonderful open spaces of
colourful Moorland.
Where the grouse when startled lift to the sky and the Deers roam
wild and free.
The gentle Does protected by the Stags, so elegant and proud
fascinate me.

I have not travelled extensively.
But there are countries I admire immensely.

Holland and Belgium hold memories dear, and I love the vastness of
France, with its wonderful race courses and marvellous fairytale
chateaux.
And for me a once in a lifetime experience was to tour the vineyards
and leisurely capture the flavour and taste of the wines.
It was a novelty I could get used to given the time.
On route I delighted in the pretty villages and the gentle sloping vine
covered hillsides.
It was plain to see they were tended lovingly with joy and pride.
At last we reached the town of Epernay, with it's elegant Avenue De
Champagne, known worldwide for its famous Champagne Houses.
It was exciting to see and hear the Champagne bottles uncorked and
being invited to sample the wine, before making a purchase.

More wine tasting sessions followed and we left Epernay light hearted
and merry.
A memorable occasion. The Wine of Celebration.

One can't journey to France without visiting the war cemeteries.
Where so many young died in two world wars, that we might live
and travel happy and free, in peace and harmony.

Elizabeth M Crellin

Seawatch

Boom, Boom, Boom.
The endless, perilous
Drum roll of the sea
Against the taut
Vellum of the cliffs
Ever pounding, ever pounding,
The heartbeat of the world.

Roll, Roll, Roll.
Onward, ever onward,
To monotony
And then beyond monotony
To patiently determined malevolence,
The dull, unabating anger of
The enemy of the world.

Pipe, Pipe, Pipe.
The wind shrieks
Its summons to the attack,
Its skirl of urging
The wavetop warriors
To heighten the assault
On the foeman, the Earth.

Rage, Rage, Rage.
The pulses race,
Another sea bastion falls
In the pounding excitement
Of another surprise raid
On the crumbling battlements
Of the encircled Earth.

Plash, Plash, Plash.
The fury abates while
With the playfulness
Of the playground bully,
The invader toys
With its reeling
Victim the Earth.

Roll, Roll, Roll.
The sea goes on forever,
A small erosion
Of determination at the front;
A retreat; an abandonment
In the infinitely untiring promenade
Of conquest of the World.

Doom, Doom, Doom.
The sea continues its rise.
The last soil in
the last garden
Will vanish,
Leaving a gently heaving
Eternity of grey water.

Ted Harriott

The Importance Of The River

The landing stage was small
With no more than six rickety steps.
In the height of summer branches
Brushed against the slippery planks
Hiding this passage from view.
Punts bobbed gently, their towing ropes
Loosely bound around a stave -
Cello notes with a chorus of bird song.
A boy and girl dangled brown legs and
Made circles, as did fish, with willow wands.

The steamer left from Folly Bridge
A few days trip to Windsor
The captain in resplendent cap
Stood at the polished wood brass wheel
Smiling at his varied passengers -
Hailing the delights they would encounter
Ifley Lock where they would tether.
Henley Races Abingdon shores -
A girl sold guide books, drinks and met
And shared her river with the Cherwell linked.

The tow path stretched for many miles
Past bridges, reeds and danger signs.
As rushing rapids forked the bend with
Water tinkling fast to flow,
Frothy billows pulling in - a small
Craft that apt to glide - towards the
Rocks and pebbles clear, would then
Collide, spilling out into the weir
Disturbing moorhen, dab-chick, coot
Confusing swans so white, so mute.

The path was baked hard sand and grit
The rushes edged the slopes and banks
Yellow flag irises glimpsed the clouds
Balsam, sweet scented filled the air
Tufty moss made cushion mounds
To sit and stare at all around, to skim
The water with pebble smooth or
Race a paper-raft against the ebb
Whilst river music sounds deluding
Caressed time away - so soothing.

At night, the girl would walk again
Along the tow paths winding light
Silvery now like jewelled thread
Precious moments flirting through her head
Her hand clasped to the boy by her side
Until they wandered, no person left
Just the swans, the dancing willows,
The mossy clumps for a pillow
They would be entwined as one
While the river smiled and shared
Its secrets with a fading sun.

Joan Richardson

Sex Symbol

Built with classic proportions'
Basically starting off with good intentions.
Beauty which is bastardised,
By a career that is jeopardised.

Maybe begun in all innocence;
Not manifested into common sense.
Attracted by the spotlight 'aura';
By a child that wasn't a horror.

An icon in an immoral society;
Where the public think them a deity.
The lifestyle takes it's toll;
As they end-up selling their soul.

Pressurised by an ever-demanding public;
The tackiness begins to stick.
Drugged into a life of submission
Unable to make a rational decision.

Un-knowing they stumble from bed to bed;
Sometimes looking as though unfed.
Unable to assimilate what they have read;
It's no wonder some end-up dead.

Alastair Buchanan

Leaves

Shadowed leaves below the canopies,
Soft greens, dark greens,
Boughs intertwining like unmarked snakes,
So much to be seen.

The high call of the birds,
Notes taken up by others,
Lost amongst the leaves,
Nesting carefully, balanced on tiny claws.

Dark green conifers reaching up to the sky,
Pale green hanging willows,
A cluster of grass and moss below,
As on the ground they grow.

Tall trunks like pillars, surrounding me,
Hundreds of different greens,
Leaves of every shade,
Comforting miracles that nature made.

Anna Parkhurst

The Silver Cage

In vain he hops from perch to perch
Wings spread, as once more he has to try
Inherited instincts from a bygone age
Telling him he was born to fly

His songs to listeners seem full of joy
But in fact they're full of pain
As he calls out to some distant mate
A union for which he calls in vain

His plumage tells of a distant land
Of sunshine and forests green
But for this poor bird is forever cursed
For that sight to remain unseen

To be used as a colourful ornament
Bought on some housewives whim
But if the position was reversed
It would be considered a major sin

But mankind's selfish and wicked ways
Has me grieving with impotent rage
As birds were meant to fly wild and free
Not be incarcerated in a silver cage

Don Woods

Timeless Seas

Pounding the earth, I watch your waves,
knowing at sea a storm does rage,
wild untamed adventurous sea
how I long to ride with thee.

Knowing of the lands, I could have seen,
watching each shore with its mystery
some so wild, out of reach,
others so calm with sparkling beach.

Eastern cities with spices rare,
and camels who just sit and stare
great are the pyramids to every eye
some hid by the sand, lost in time.

Risking the danger of your tides
on your back I would take that ride,
impressive, in a storm you rave
sending, many to their grave.

The earth you batter very hard
often, she is caught off guard,
displacing rocks from the land
rolling together, in the sand.

Untamed that beauty it draws me,
and many others to your sea,
like some toy you stay, or play
then so bored you roll away.

We cannot master this timeless sea,
you hold our love with your mystery,
yet risking all dangers I would ride
to see this world, by your side.

Naomi Ruth Whiting

Like A Bird

Have you ever lay in a field and watched the clouds float by?
Have you ever watched a bird fly by?
Have you ever wished you were that bird which flies so high in the
sky?
And watched it swoop back down to earth to land in trees, or on the
ground? Looking for food all around.

Have you ever wondered what it would be like to eat a worm? or a
fly?
To scamper around on the ground to look for seed that can't be
found.

Have you ever wondered what it would be like to sleep in trees in the
dead of night?
When the snow falls all around, and all the worms lie frozen in the
ground, and you feel too cold and weak to fly around?
Then in the morning when you awoke you heard a blackbird burst
into song, and announce the down has come.
You knew at once that spring is here.
Your cold, chilled body began to thaw, and all the snow began to
melt.
All the other birds that were around began their mating in the trees.
They were on the ground, they were in the air, they seemed to be
mating everywhere.
They were building nests to raise their young.
You sat and wondered if you'd be next to find a loved and build your
nest to raise your young
And watch them fly high in the sky and swoop back down to the
ground.
Well have you ever wondered what it would be like?
I have.

R Anderton

All You Want Is Love

Baby gurgling in your pram,
Lifting up your dimpled hands,
Kicking both your tiny feet,
Little baby, soft and sweet.

Why are you so happy,
When the rest of us are sad?
What can you see baby dear
That keeps your heart so glad?

Perhaps you see the angels still,
Perhaps you understand,
Perhaps you hold God's heaven
In your tiny hand.

And perhaps you see the truth
When we see just a lie,
For all you ask is someone kind
To kiss you when you cry.

And all you want are singing birds,
And the dancing swaying leaves,
But we have grown greedy
And are not content with these.

So no wonder you are happy
Like a gentle coo-ing dove,
For you still see the beauty
And all you want is love.

Jenny Eleftheriades

The Pub

    I am a counsellor.
I can give you comfort, warmth and joy.
Encapsulated in the four walls that are me
I am a mother for every girl and boy
With suckling babies in their hundreds.
My breasts are full of ale
With liquids for the young and old
And spirits for those in between.

    I am a discotheque.
With me are machines which bellow out the sweetest music.
Whilst you listen to it
I'll help you burp, but not be weaned.

    I am shelter
From the elements, when the North wind blows
And we shall have snow.
What will the robbers do then?
When they arrive
I've a tasty hot-pot for them.

    I have a hiding place
For persons good and bad.
A refuge for husbands and foolish sons
Whose wives and girlfriends
Through their mouths
Have made them sad.

    I am a dating agency
For all who enter in.
Many will lose in their search for love
But quite often one or two will win.

I am a crystal ball.
Look at me and you will see
Footballers, clergymen and models
Housewives and husbands
All wanting to watch a film or a match.
However come to me quite regularly
And you will look like you will soon
Have something to hatch.

I am a department store
With glasses and furniture in display.
I am a supermarket with nibbles
For which I assure you
You will have to pay!

J Robinson

Mount Kinabalu

When we first caught a glimpse of the mountain ahead
A woman regarded it briefly and said,
'I'll find a hotel and leave mountains to you
For there's no way that I can climb Kinabalu.'

The rain that had fallen the previous day
Had carried a lot of the footpath away,
But we made our way up through the jungle that grew
On the slopes near the base of Mount Kinabalu.

The pathway was sunk under slime-covered roots
That offered poor holds for our track shoes or boots
And often we feared that our feet would slip through
To the ooze underneath on Mount Kinabalu.

There were shelters with seats where we'd gratefully sink
To snatch a short rest while we took a quick drink,
And then we'd continue and all we could do
Was keep slogging on up Mount Kinabalu.

The way became steeper, the country more bare,
And the wind on the heights brought a chill to the air.
Then we stopped at a hut for a meal and a brew
And a bunk for the night on Mount Kinabalu.

We rose in the dark and set off about four;
It was bitterly cold and beginning to pour,
And the group who had started was now minus two
Who fell out on the way up Mount Kinabalu.

Our torches cast wavering patches of light
That did little to brighten the gloom of the night,
But we scrambled and clambered and steadily drew
Nearer the top of Mount Kinabalu.

The tour agent's staff had misled us a bit
By saying we needn't bring ropes in our kit,
And I have to admit it was perfectly true -
They were hung from the rocks on Mount Kinabalu.

Like spiders we climbed as we clung to a rope
And traversed on the almost precipitous slope
On a ledge scarcely more than the width of a shoe
Way up on the side of Mount Kinabalu.

But a little while later we came to a stop
To watch the sun rise as we stood on the top
And the light of the dawn showed a breath-taking view
Spread out all around below Kinabalu.

Iris Metcalfe

A Day Is Born

Gone the shroud of darkness,
Light filters through the air.
The rising sun
A crimson flare,
Brings in on cue
The feathered choir.

Dew, a diamond carpet
Covers all the land.
Unseen the cuckoo
Calls with mirth,
Bushes laced with cobwebs
Night has given birth.

Joan Blake

Colours

Blue, so exquisite, blue of the skies,
Blue of the bluebell, blue, babies eyes.
Green of the grass and emerald ring,
Green of the new leaves early in Spring.
Red of the sunset's glow in the West,
Red of the rose, and blithe robin's breast.

Pink of the piglet, squealing in sty,
Pink tipped each bud when summer is nigh.
Yellow, bright buttercups, 'round my feet,
Yellow of baby chicks, fluffy, sweet.
Brown of the earth and my true love's eyes,
Brown the crisp pastry on tasty pies.

Russet of apples ripening on trees,
Russet, autumn leaves blown by the breeze.
Golden the cornfields, golden the sand,
Golden sunflowers, daffodil band.
Grey of the smart suits he likes to wear,
Grey now the colour turning our hair.

White of a snowflake, fragile and light,
White, wedding gown, a beautiful sight.
Deep purple shadows when evening falls,
Deep purple velvet, funeral palls.
Black raven's wing and coal of black jet,
Black ebony, new tar gleaming, wet.

Silvery raindrops, stars shining bright,
Silver the moonbeams glimm'ring by night.
Contrasting colours playing a part
Bringing their mem'ries into the heart
Without colours life would be bleak, for
Where would Rose hide in baby's soft cheek?

Joan Heybourn

Echoes

The echo of your presence fill this empty room
The loudness of the silence is with me now,
Laughter's gone for ever, for me there's only gloom,
Bereft am I, shadows assail me now.

The sunshine of your presence, turned to bleakest night,
Emptiness surrounds me now,
You left, and took away my light,
Life's not worth living now.

Still though, in the silence that once you filled,
I seem to hear a whisper, that comes upon me now,
An echo of the time you loved, but now is still'd,
The past is done, but it is with me now . . .

R Caswell

Hold The Moment

The wheels are turning on the train
Homeward bound I am
The holiday is over
But my feet still tread the sand
I can smell the clear sea breeze
Feel the water lapping
Hear the screeching gulls above
See the children clapping
The Punch and Judy Show
Granddads with trousers rolled
Holding hands with grans paddling
Eyes the colour of sea and sky
And a feel of a kiss goodbye!

J E Veazey

When Your Luck Ain't So Good

If money be your god
Catch a devil by the tail;
For a shilling sell your soul,
For a penny end in jail;

As this devil has no friends,
Till the time his bidding's done,
And tread you upon that fiery trail,
Then you and he are one!

But wayward we all are,
And our vices we possess;
Some pity is kept in short supply,
If no balance we redress.

But can we keep that ill at bay?
Are there wise men there to see;
Whose fiddle plays a better tune
For the likes of you and me?

And those preachers in their den,
Will they come out and tell us when
Their words of wisdom we can thank,
When we've just got empty pockets,
    and nothing in the bank?

Alistair McLean

Winter Journeys

Footsteps crunching through freshly fallen snow,
Ducks breaking the ice on their frozen pond.
Breath coming out in clouds as on I go,
My destination lying far beyond.

Passing through the forest with trees so bare,
Animals hiding safely in their den.
Walking further on and I'm almost there,
Opening the door now I'm home again.

Looking out the window at the snowflakes,
Sky getting darker now that night is near.
Watching a man as frozen steps he takes,
Turning up the fire, glad that I'm in here.

Kaz

A Jewel - So Precious

Love is - a look across a crowded room,
A smile beyond compare,
It hits you like a sonic boom,
The real thing - alas - all too rare!

Love is - the feeling you are walking on air,
Every moment just magic - with more in store,
Dinner by candlelight - soft music to share,
A kiss - a caress - as never before!

Love is - the laughter that abounds every day,
A heartbeat missed whenever you meet,
Can this wonderful feeling really be here to stay,
To be cared for - and care so - is no small feat!

Jill M Ronald

I Haven't A Clue

Ideas, inspirations, they're all around,
The problem is - where are they to be found!
Poets like Yeats could go round for many-a-day,
Without saying anything - in a poetic way!
They'd sit looking glum with nothing to do,
Where are inspirations to be found - I haven't a clue!!

G Carbery

Clouds

Those moving, sailing, flying clouds
In my memory they sing loud.
When a little child, then my fancy
Was so lively, I felt happy.

I believed the clouds were real lands
And I was taken to far islands.
Life prevents me from looking up,
Living carefree . . . I've to give up.

Now I've grown older, am I wiser?
The clouds move on higher, farther,
I wish men dropped no killing clouds
Hiroshima is crying loud.

P Jean

Casting The First Stone

You cry for peace
But mine is the war party.
Bitterness and destruction course through my veins
As surely as mercy and moderation
Patrol the boundaries of your impartial judgements.

Yours the bewilderment
For children violated,
Innocence obliterated,
Death delivered with designer labelling.
Mine the steady shame of self knowledge.

Francesca Tyrrell

Nairobi

A muzzled dog at the garden gate tries vainly to bay at the moon.

The jacarandas lean like long-legged model girls, waiting
appointments.

Cloud-cuckoos twitter all night long at a pile of fag-ends in a
gleaming tray.

In the Rift Valley the arching sky holds eagles, crying alleluia,

And stringy marsh birds chitter chatter, their scissor-beaks pinking
the shore.

Nairobi's mono high life drones on and on; a second full-length
movie feature . . . .
Celluloid dolphins in the new hotels nuzzle promiscuous quays.

Yet only twenty miles away the waxing moon fingers the hills with
more than moonlight.

Harriet Jillings

Anya

A friend of mine asked me to write,
a poem about her nice pink bike.
I can't think what on earth to put,
as I met Anya whilst on foot.
She loves the wheels, the seat and colour
and journeys far to make life fuller.
If only I could pen great words,
about this thing that glides like birds.
Instead I sit and wonder why,
a girl would want to cycle by,
a brook, a forest down the lane,
all green and lovely in the rain.
A milestone that is overgrown,
a crow that from the nest has flown
and in the hedgerow now is peeping,
a dainty flower and green frog leaping.
A rainbow and a cuckoo's song,
are found above brown furrows long.
The glory of a silent day,
is there when Anya speeds away
from lands that once were England's glory,
but now become a textbook story.
The wild woodbine and blossom white,
have nearly vanished out of sight!
Keep riding till at last one day,
the woodlands do then pass away.
Your bright pink bike is but a dream,
for all the things that it has seen.

Tom Clarke

King Of The Road

Perhaps if like me you commute in your car, you'll know that I'm
                                        right to declare
That drivers with manners and sense at the wheel are becoming
                                        increasingly rare.

The numbers are growing of clowns who ignore, as if they've a God
                                        given right,
The speed limit zones, and with foot on the floor overtake all the
                                        traffic in sight.

And I've often encountered in fog or in snow or when driving at
                                        night in the rain,
Identical cretins who cannae go slow, and wished I was safe on the
                                        train.

Conversely there's those who sedately progress, relaxed and
                                        apparently blind
To the mounting impatience, frustration, and stress that they cause to
                                        the drivers behind.

Commuting means potholes and roadworks and spray, and traffic in
                                        lines nose to stern,
And lorries and buses that get in the way, and morons who
                                        winker-less turn.

And driving at night with your motor unlit or on sidelights alone is a
                                        crime,
Yet, like misaligned headlamps that dazzle on dip, I meet with it all of
                                        the time.

It's few who are free of the faults I discern, and journeys would
                                        pleasanter be
If all would admit it and set out to learn how to drive right and
                                        proper - like me.

So study your foibles my friend and contrive, on accepting the truth
                                        of this Ode,
To exercise patience and caution, and strive to act like a Knight of the
                                        Road.

There's one final rule to observe when it's clear you're with elegant
driving au fait,
Keep using your mirror and when I appear . . . Kowtow and get out
of my way!

Alan Ayre

High Tide At Southend

The estuarine waters ooze in over the flaccid mud,
Bait diggers retreat before the advancing flood
And leave the ragworm to their cool and silky homes.
Now the slick waves slip and slap across the bones
Of rotting hulks and ships long dead that in a by-gone age
Rode the proud oceans of the world and faced the rage
Of battering storms, the decks awash, the mast-head bare
And now lie dreaming in their muddy bed of zephyrs fair.

Now when the tide of life is at the full, the sun
Sparkles on the open sea and our hearts still run
With the youth who sets his board before the breeze.
Then rather than retire before the flood we take the seas
Head on, ride out the tempest and brave the doldrums drear,
Nor backward cast the eye, nor be engulfed in fear,
But keep the helm before the mark, our eyes upon the star
That to our haven brings us, safely past the bar.

John Stanbridge

The Dream

I stood in awe
I heard the roar
The roar of rolling thunder.

Transfixed with fear
I could not move
The ship was torn asunder.

When I awoke
The sea was calm
I saw the morning glory.
Only driftwood passing by
Told the awful story.

My lips were cracked
My body ached
None but dead around me.
They come now one by one
The killer sharks surrounds me.

Isabel McEwing

Hidden Paths

Timelessness surrounds you, you who are always near,
Many seasons have passed since meeting face to face,
Nothing within has changed.
Yours is a face that haunts, eloquent, expressive eyes
That transmitted volumes without uttering a word,
As deep inside I stirred.

When your voice spoke to mine, mine gave answering echo,
Inwardly filled with joy at such discovery rare
As mingling of two souls.
From that moment onward it was not important
Which words were spoken, but that shudder of joy
Priceless, beyond compare.

The artist's slender hand, beautiful tone of voice,
Your nature revealing that gentle disposition,
Encircling, drawing close.
I cannot deny yearning with desire for you,
When you gazed on me, lost in a kiss or embrace,
Trembling in ecstasy.

Whenever you were near how my happiness soared,
Now alone with sadness, feelings for you unchanged,
Came discovery of pain.
Your image before me, a photograph acquired,
Reminder of you ever graven on my heart,
It's a comfort to hold.

Continuing as before as if nothing had changed,
Inner feelings hidden while duties I perform;
But I know what is true.
Following path of duty, despite desire strong,
Believe love never fades, although unacknowledged,
True love always endures.

Love always a wonder, even in deepest grief,
Lovely cherished gift, highest pinnacle of life,
Love everywhere, yet free.
If love is life's meaning there will be no regret,
Earthly living and dying but steps on the way
Towards eternity.

Betty Mealand

The Birthday

The old man walked with ferrets in his trousers
His teeth rattled and jiggered when he talked
Short of breath he stopped and fingered the air
'I'm eighty today!'
Even though he forgot his bus fare
'I'm eighty today!'
Whatever the family may say
Sometimes he forgets who he is
But that doesn't matter
For he will learn anew

Paul Andrew Jones

The Futile Ones

We all have a basic need to be noticed and to make our presence
                                                          known.
However, there are members of some families that parents would just
                                                          as soon disown.
Being born with a natural desire for challenge it presents itself in
                                                          different ways.
In fact some go to extremes to get noticed - disrupt and vandalise
                                                          even on their better days.
You would think parents of someone so irresponsible - that one they
                                                          would despise.
In fact if they condone such outrageous behaviour it could be the
                                                          whole family has much to revise.
We see programmes where some admit to actually enjoying it all and
                                                          to get a buzz that we just can't believe.
How could there be such a despicable offspring that any mother
                                                          could conceive.
Ironically a member of that family could be in need of the very phone
                                                          that they put out of action.
They could be injured, or even dying, deserving no charitable
                                                          re-action.
There are even instances where doctors and nurses are abused and
                                                          prevented from even attending to life saving care.
Possibly by this very family who would demand that Samaritans have
                                                          time to spare.
If only we could segregate those who destroy the very amenity that is
                                                          shared by most of us.
And they did not have the help they are undeserving of - by our
                                                          carers - perhaps it would be a plus.

Reg Morris

Alice's Soul

Slip, sliding it on to her tongue,
'For a bit of a laugh, just some fun'
Everyone said, it was the 'Thing' to do.
Now she thought, she would do it too.
When friends came by, she was feeling high.
She started to cry, but she didn't know why!
'I'm Alice,' she sobbed, 'I'm slipping down a hole.'
'Don't let me fall, I will meet my soul.'
She was taken out to the cool fresh air.
All she could do was to sit, and stare.
As night moved on, she slipped down the hole,
Slip, slip, Sliding to meet her soul.

Sue White

Nature's Treasures

Fragrant of the apple blossom makes the day.
Clouds of mist rise from the valley floor.
Wooded valley with hundreds of bluebells
Glittering with cheer.
Old oak shelters the fox from bitter wind,
Buttercups give nectar to our honey bees
Gathering for the long winter ahead.
Blustering wind shakes everything into tempting hibernation.

Alan Hattersley

Momentum

Don't stop for a moment
life is rushing by
you need to try and catch it
time is not a lie.
Think at double quick pace
churn out words of work
look at people in the face
and challenge what they do.
Faster, faster than the rest
race the team-mates to touch the line
drive speedily and pass the test
win, win, never fail.

What happens if we slow it all down?
Will life really end?
Will anyone really notice
if we stop the momentum for a rest?

Cath Spooner

Nice Boy Next Door

He was always different from the other boys, affectionate and kind,
They never seemed to accept him, but he didn't seem to mind,
But his happy times ended, when he started school,
He found it difficult to learn, and the other kids called him a fool.
He struggled on for ages, never stayed at home when he was sick,
But he still couldn't learn, even the teachers said he was thick.

Then one day he came home from school, smiling happily,
And said, 'I got a new teacher today, and he knows what's wrong
                                                    with me.'
They said he was dyslexic, word blindness it was called,
That's why he couldn't read or write, or understand what was on the
                                                    blackboard.
Of course that changed everything, and he went from strength to
                                                    strength,
He tried to learn everything, he would go to any length.
Eventually he went off to college, and took a law degree,
Now I read about him in the papers, or watch him on TV.

He still pops around to see us, his head up, full of pride,
And a lot of those kids that laughed at him, ended up inside.

Maureen Arnold

Pollution

People pollute our wonderful planet
Our gift from God and we try to destroy it
Living as though there is no tomorrow
Littering, degrading and showing no sorrow
Under the threat of nuclear destruction
Towards oblivion amidst ignorant confusion
I trust some day we'll come to our senses
Our whole world scrapping, all their defences
And mankind enjoying the beauty that lies
Between land and water and our heavenly skies
Start looking around just think what it's worth
Nothing can match our life here on earth.

R McFarlane

Thirty Pieces Of Silver

For thirty pieces of silver,
Judas betrayed His Master
Peter a favourite disciple denied Jesus thrice,
declaring and swearing
he never knew the Master,

Jesus the meek shepherd of the sheep
betrayed again by Judas,
With a mocking kiss on the cheek.
The scoffing sign for Roman soldiers
to take hold of Jesus.
Leading Him away to be crucified
on the cross at Calvary.
Judas ran into the temple
filled with shame and despair
throwing the thirty pieces of silver
on the temple floor.
When he found no one did care
Judas who betrayed the Son of the Living God
could live with himself no more,
he sealed his awful doom
going out the temple door.
Thirty pieces of silver lay scattered
on the temple floor,
Judas went out and hanged himself
his guilt he could stand no more.
Jesus was denied, betrayed, crucified.
The Price He paid His blood was shed,
at a place called Calvary.
We are bought at a price.
The price of Jesus precious Blood.

Frances Gibson

Shouldn't You?

Like a star in the sky that shines
Or a smile through a breaking heart
To unwind through teeth that grind
A cry of joy while it's falling apart.

To treat life as a gift, which isn't a myth
To break the key to your heart from its chain
Feelings are for showing with eyes to see with
To spiritually feel like a child again.

Adapt to a world that is blind
God knows you can't change everyone
There's a path which is not hard to find
Take the first step, unite with the sun.

Love is alive, it's free and it's real
Misery and sadness are extortionate in price
Look into your mind as I know how you feel
Destroy the mask friend and think twice.

Mhairi Hamilton

The Big Sale - A Sorry Tale

The tax payers know it's not fair,
Nearly all MPs end up millionaires
The last PM let down and ditch,
Wrote a book that made her rich,
We old 'uns would like to see,
The MPs live on money like the OAPs.
I dare say one MP would try,
All the bills and food to buy,
Give up your lifestyle for just a year,
Live in a council flat without a beer,
Don't forget the poll-tax did fail,
And put a few innocent people in jail,
OAP's quality of life,
Just ask a few of Britain's housewives,
Saying it could be made better,
Honest truth as I write this letter,
They don't get much that is free,
Licence in Australia on TV you see
British people will not let it rest - All the sell-offs
(Will save NHS).

T Blaney

Say It With Flowers - This Way!

Lily of the Valley, white, Jewish High Priest.
Bluebells, blue on white, Mother Mary!
Cat ho licks, don't protest, Ebor ices-cold?!
'Flower-girls - it is dull today, but sunny, better tomorrow' - ?!

'Ouvre la fênestra, le porte, dans le jardin tout!'
'Faith, hope and Charity' - St Paul Corinthians 12

Janet N Edwards

Remembering Friends

Friendship in life, our greatest gift
No-one should be without.
The shaken hand of trust and love
The cool hand that soothes the brow
Someone who aids, when all goes wrong.
Who tends you when you're ill
Someone to lift your spirits
When life's problems pull you down.

True friendship has a meaning
A human vessel filled with love
Someone who seeks to aid you
To pacify your mind.
To hold the hand that trembles
With the worries of mankind
A friend, the shadow by your side
No-one should be without.
Who always stays beside you
To remove your fears and doubts.

To me my wife is my best friend
Always standing by my side.
Her arms outstretched to aid me
True friendship at my side.

Leslie Rushbury

Untitled

Oh let me wander, once again
Hand in hand with a love
Talking in whispers, not to detain
A fox, rabbit or bird in flight
Listening to trees, whispering in a breeze
My love holding me close to his side
We can hear the hum of the thresher
Collecting the corn from the fields
Then to that oak we carefully lean
As silent passion consumes us.
Oh please let me wander, just once more
In that quiet woodland glade.

Winifred Parkinson

Summer Magic

What was that sound? I stepped from the path
And peered into the dark fastness of woodland,
I heard the faint chimes of a clock in a distant tower.
The evening shadows hid an army of creatures
Moving around me. The soft wing of a moth touched my face.
Then, in the still air, the stirrings ceased, the wood fell silent,
There was a strange excitement of anticipation,
As from a nearby bush came a plaintive cluster of notes,
An evocative call tossed in the air, a flow of melody
Piped as from a faery flute. The wood was bewitched
By the sound. Even the screech owls were silent.

The nightingale pursued his overture, trilling gently
As he composed the song for us. Short bursts of phrases
Interspersed with silences floated through the night air.
Then a brilliant cascade became a sparkling allegro,
A tumbling of notes from the very heart of the singer.
Immersed in the sound, I recalled the echoes
Of a vanished horizon, the world in the passin of its youth.
The song pouring from primeval woods into the new Millennium
Now upon us; the same sound, the offering of the bird
To its creator. A gift of love, indeed.

Lost in my thoughts in the beauty of the scene,
The litany of praise was fading into silence.
The woodland creatures resumed their nightly foraging,
I heard the soft brushing of feet and the harsh cry of a vixen.
In a daze I retraced my steps in the moonlight,
The clear plaintive notes still fresh in my ears.
A symphony of joy in the thrill of being alive
From a little brown bird on a sweet summer night.

Beryl Louise Penny

Spring Has Sprung

The cuckoo comes in April
At least that's what is told
And everywhere around us
The world is turning gold
There's lots of yellow crocuses
And daffodils so tall
With little golden primroses
Against the garden wall
So please do look around you
The world is good to see
With lots of yellow catkins
On green and budding trees.

Sheila Elkins

Sun

You bring your light to earth each day,
Then silently you steal away.
So constant and without fail,
As revered as the holy grail.

No pilgrim more alone than thee,
As travelled over land or sea.
And though your work is never done,
Welcome to thee oh friend called sun.

You travel on as nations sleep;
Thy covenant with God to keep.
No human claims they fealty;
You shine on mans inadequacy.

So wanderer over every shore,
Keep thee thy secrets evermore.
A greater power guides thee thy way;
To serve a miracle of day.

W Hopkins

Scotland Is Mine

Beautiful Scotland
you are here to stay
in our hearts and memory
as one can only say.

Wonderful in the sunshine you stand
where men can still find lots of friends.
Treasures old and new
with misty days more than a few.

The beaches and hills
blue and green, the colours full fill
what's nowhere else
to be seen.

The castles and hotels
are rich and all-round
and sometimes you can hit your head for dreaming
on the ground.

Legends and true fairytales
the mystique and romance
is so real
you want to dance.

If you are looking to find your fortune
don't look any further
it shouldn't depend on the weather!
And we have the most glorious heather.

    Ria Probst

Mirrored Dreams

Into a galaxy of fantasy,
Controlled by joys divine,
In dreams I reach to far extremes,
Beyond the fringe of time.

In dreams to once upon a times,
Down the avenues of truth,
The seasons of my life I tread,
On pathways of my youth.

On pillowed calm of fantasy,
Sedated by the night,
In dreams I vision happiness,
Where peace and love unite.

Malcolm Wilson Bucknall

Romany Rue

Oh yes! She weaved her magic spell,
This Romany woman in gypsy dress,
And when on me her eyes did dwell,
I felt I needed her caress.

Posed on one leg, the other on heel tip,
Thick, curly dark hair flecked with grey,
Red skirt awhirl with shake of hip,
The hands eloquent in aerial display.

Her blouse of white with stripes of blue,
Full of sleeve and edged with lace,
Dark waistcoat embroidered with every hue,
Serene the smile on that proud face.

I am sure those dark eyes held a sign,
But too soon my gypsy figure went away,
Leaving me bereft, on my own to pine,
My heart empty, but the pictures stay.

Gordon Jack Crisp